COPYRIGHT NOTICE

Get Speaking Gigs Now is protected by copyright law. The contents of this book may not be reproduced or transmitted in any form or by any means, electronic or mechanical, including photocopying, recording or by any information storage and retrieval system without written permission from the author, except for the inclusion of brief quotations in a review.

© 2020-2023 BY LEISA REID
ALL RIGHTS RESERVED WORLDWIDE
ISBN-13: 978-1676914341

For more information about **Get Speaking Gigs Now**; individual orders; bundled orders, discounts for bulk-quantity purchases; audio products; interviews; information on seminars; JV opportunities; mentoring/consulting; booking the author to speak at your next seminar, workshop or event; please contact Leisa at her website:

www.GetSpeakingGigsNow.com

INCOME DISCLAIMER: Every effort has been made to accurately represent the subject nature of this book and all its potential. Even though most industries are ones where a person can "write their own ticket" in terms of earning potential, there is "no guarantee" that you will earn any money using the teachings, lessons and ideas found in this book. Any examples provided are not to be interpreted as a promise or guarantee of earnings. Earning potential is entirely dependent upon the sincere effort and the effective use of what is found in this book and on your own individual effort, circumstances and more. That said, here's to your success.

LEISA REID

TABLE OF CONTENTS

Message From The Author

Forward

PART 1
Get Your Talk Ready to Rock

PART 2
Create Your Ideal Speaking Gig Pipeline

PART 3
Monetize Your Speaking Engagements

PART 4
Systems To Getting Asked Back Again & Again

PART 5
Speaker Sheet Development You'll Need

PART 6
Keeping Your Speaking Gig Pipeline FULL

PART 7
Scripts For Getting Booked & Staying Booked

Summary / Wrap-Up

Back Pages

ABOUT THE AUTHOR

LEISA REID

Whether you are a speaker or not, there is no doubt we all have an expertise that can leave an impact on the world once it is shared.

As founder of a company that helps speakers "Get Speaking Gigs Now," Leisa Reid mentors business professionals and entrepreneurs who want to make an impact and ultimately attract their ideal clients through speaking.

As a speaker herself, Leisa has successfully booked and delivered over 500 speaking engagements. She is passionate about training speakers with varying levels of experience, messages, and niche markets. She believes a great foundation, solid network, and proven strategies can help propel speakers to actualizing their potential.

In addition to being a professional speaker and coach, Leisa earned both a Bachelors and a Masters degree in Speech Communication. When she was just 22 years old, she taught Interpersonal Communication classes at California State University, Fullerton.

She has lived in Orange County, California since 1991 after moving from her hometown of Fairbanks, Alaska.

MESSAGE FROM THE AUTHOR

I believe everyone has a story to tell. We all have experiences, memories, expertise and lessons we have learned that can benefit other people.

I LOVE the experience of when a "talk" comes to me. It's as if a seed was planted and it starts to grow. It can even wake me up in the middle of the night!

You've probably had a similar experience of having a "talk" come to you and start to grow within you. You may have watched another speaker on stage and thought, "I could be up there!"

It's an exciting time to be a business owner or entrepreneur with a powerful message. Why? Because you can carve out your own way in the speaking world. All you need is the willingness and courage to go for it! Oh yeah, and a message that is worthy of sharing.

It is my honor to be on this journey with you! One of the messages I have received is that I am on this planet to share my knowledge in service of transformation for others.

I believe we are all connected, and I have knowledge that can help you get your message heard so you can help other people, and on and on. The ripple effect has begun!

FORWARD BY

BART SMITH
BARTSMITHWORLD.COM
AUTHOR / SPEAKER / TRAINER

As a professional speaker, and author of **99+ Speaking Success Tactics**, Leisa is spot on with her approach to "getting more speaking gigs!"

When I first met Leisa, I was so impressed with her speaking accomplishments and then when I learned that she founded *OC Speakers Network* (600+ members) based in Capistrano Beach, CA, a support group for speakers, I was even more drawn to what she had to offer.

With over 500 booked and delivered speaking engagements, Leisa is certainly the go-to person to learn how to "get more speaking gigs!" What speaker doesn't want more opportunities to speak? We all do!

Having read through this book and reviewed her "Get Speaking Gigs Now" training program, it's obvious Leisa has what it takes to help every eager speaker *"get more speaking gigs!"*

PART I

GET YOUR TALK READY TO ROCK

Get more speaking gigs when you train at GetSpeakingGigsNow.com ...

PART 1 – GET YOUR TALK READY TO ROCK

Q: What does it mean to get your talk ready to rock?

There is nothing like the feeling of speaking in front of an audience and being IN FLOW.

1. **The audience is engaged and leaning in,** you are in the zone, feeling confident and there is a feeling of ease, certainty, buzz in the air.

2. **People come up to you afterwards** and are interested in your services or business offerings.

3. **They tell you how much they were affected by what you said** and they would like to learn more about you and what you offer.

4. **They ask if you might be able to help them** because they can relate to what you shared.

Throughout this experience ... you were YOU! You spoke from a place of authenticity, truth and shared your expertise in a way that felt truly in alignment with who you are. The audience felt that from you.

You knew where you were taking the audience because you had intentionally created your talk with them in mind. You narrowed down your years of expertise into bite-size pieces that they could understand. You made the pathway to working with you super clear and easy without sounding or feeling "salesy." It felt natural. You remembered to share your call to action and kept it clear and easy for the audience to make a decision. You did that confidently because, again, you were intentional and prepared.

You had practiced your talk so that your anxiety level was low and your confidence, certainty and connection with the audience shone through. People felt that. You were a ROCK STAR!

Network with other speakers! Go to GetSpeakingGigsNow.com/network

That is what I mean when I help people get their talks ready to ROCK. No two talks are alike because no two speakers are alike. It's not about being someone else. It's about YOU and your expertise and how you can make the biggest impact with the time you have on stage.

Q: How do you know you are ready to get your talk ready to rock and become a speaker?

You are ready if you are:

1. **Pushing speaking opportunities away** because you're working on your talk.

I see this SO often. Speakers are "working" on their talk for a loooong time. It's hard to edit our talks and narrow down our expertise because we think it's ALL important. We want to impart ALL of our knowledge. "Working on your talk" is also an excuse not to get out there and give it. It can be scary to be a speaker.

2. **Scheduled to speak**, but dreading it.

I get all kinds of 9-1-1 calls from speakers. The best advice (if you haven't done this yet) is to get help sooner rather than later! There is a way to lower all of that anxiety and make this a fun experience (and get clients too!).

One day, I got a panicked call from a woman who was scheduled to speak in front of an audience of 100 people. She was hoping they would cancel her as a speaker, because she was so nervous. The talk she had prepared didn't feel natural to her. By the time we worked together (four days before her talk – nail biter!), she was calm and felt grounded. Oh, and she did a great job!

3. **Want to use speaking** to build your business and gain clients.

Get more speaking gigs when you train at GetSpeakingGigsNow.com ...

Speaking is a fun and powerful way to attract the ideal clients who you can help. The audience has gotten insight into your personality and knowledge, so the people who resonate with you come forward. For those of us who enjoy teaching, coaching, mentoring, training and facilitating, speaking is the cat's meow! You can easily formulate a valuable talk that serves the audience AND helps you gain clients.

4. **Booked to speak** in the future.

Some of us become speakers unexpectedly. You may have experienced people asking you to speak at an event even though you weren't actively looking for the opportunity. So now what do you do? The date is looming and you still need to figure out the best way to leverage the opportunity.

This happened to one of my clients who had a fear of speaking. She is a very educated and powerful coach, but was not confident in public speaking due to English being her second language.

We found a way for her to give a powerful talk (loaded with some experiential exercises) that accented her depth and wisdom. Instead of overfeeding the audience with facts, she was able to inspire and connect through her authentic gifts as a coach.

Q: What will happen if your talk isn't ready?

Typically, there are 5 PITFALLS you can fall into when your talk isn't ready to rock.

PITFALL #1
You will push opportunities away subconsciously.

EXAMPLE: Someone says they would be interested in having you speak to their group. You say you'll email them to follow-up, but you forget to follow-up and the lead goes cold.

PITFALL #2

You will give excuses to turn down speaking opportunities.

You tell people you're still working on your talk, but it's not ready yet. You are too busy with (FILL IN THE BLANK), but you are going to finish it really soon.

PITFALL #3

You'll just WING it.

This is probably the WORST thing you can do. Winging it can be worse than not speaking at all. Why? Imagine if you drove a car for the first time by winging it. You would never do that, right? When you wing it, the audience can feel it. They are wondering where you are taking them. They can sense your anxiety and lack of confidence. It's painful for everyone.

PITFALL #4

You will miss out on client opportunities (and $$$$).

The longer you wait to get your talk ready to rock, the more opportunities you miss to utilize the "ONE-TO-MANY" approach and impact a lot of people all at once.

PITFALL #5

Most importantly, you will NOT be making the impact that you were meant to make.

Speaking can scale your business quickly and effectively. It's SO exciting, so let's make sure you get on the fast track and start making an impact.

Get more speaking gigs when you train at GetSpeakingGigsNow.com ...

PART 1 – GET YOUR TALK READY TO ROCK

Q: How do you go about getting your talk ready to rock?

There is a road map I use when coaching speakers on getting their talk ready to rock. Below is an overview so you can see the flow of the process.

- Start with the end in mind ... what is your desired end result?
- Develop compelling learning points ...
- Write a brief description of the presentation ...
- Create an attractive / enticing presentation title ...
- Practice the heck out of your presentation ...
- Outline how you would expand/shrink it ...
- Repurpose it ...

What is the desired result you want at the end of your talk?

When you are getting your talk ready to rock, a lot of emphasis is put on the content so that you know WHAT you're going to share.

BUT ...

You also need to know WHY you're going to share what you're going to share.

What is your desired end result?

- To sell WHAT product / service?
- To build your list?
- To register people to your event?
- To get more speaking engagements?

Network with other speakers! Go to GetSpeakingGigsNow.com/network

- To get clients?
- To help people with _____?

How will your talk support that desired result?

- What will you ask for at the end?
- What are you guiding the audience to do?
- What paperwork / system do you need in place?
- Where in your presentation will this happen?

What is your CTA (Call-To-Action)?

What will you ask people to do before you leave the stage? Here are some examples of what you can invite people to do:

- Continue your learning by _____ ...
- Work with you on a deeper level by _____ ...
- Overcome their challenge of _____ by _____ ...
- Solve the problems of _____ by _____ ...

Q: How do you develop compelling learning points?

Think about the main 3-5 things you tell people about your industry or expertise. What is interesting about what you offer? What you know?

For example, what are the myths / problems / solutions you:

- Tell people about ...
- Educate your clients on ...
- Post on social media ...

Get more speaking gigs when you train at GetSpeakingGigsNow.com ...

Try writing 3 learning points for yourself here:

1. _____

_____

2. _____

_____

3. _____

_____

Q: Why do you need a brief description of your talk?

A description of your talk is needed for three important reasons:

#1: You will be **asked for it by meeting planners so they can get an idea of what your talk is about** and if it's a fit for their audience.

#2: You will want to **have the description visible on your speaker sheet** (see PART VI on Speaker Sheet Development to learn more). Again, this if for the eyes of meeting planners to get an idea if your talk is a fit for their audience.

#3: When you do get booked, the **meeting planner will often highlight you in their invitations** (e.g., e-newsletter, social media, website, agenda, etc.).

Q: Why do you need an attractive title?

Your title is often the last item you define when getting your talk ready to rock. It starts to emerge as the learning points are created and the description is written. It must encompass the theme of what you're sharing as well as be catchy and/or compelling to both the meeting planner and the audience. Many times I've been told that people came to the event just to hear me speak based on the title and description of my talk.

Q: How much do you need to practice your talk?

It depends ... on how quickly you get comfortable and flow with the message you want to share. I don't mean the comfort level of the topic, I mean the comfort level of the words and the actual pacing of what you are sharing.

For example, I saw one speaker give her talk with her notes in her hand the entire time, AND she had a PowerPoint presentation. What did that tell me? That she did not take the time to practice incorporating comfort and flow into her presentation. Why? Because she was too scared to let go of her notes, it massively affected her credibility.

This is definitely one area you have in your hands to control. You can practice for free! You can practice multiple times. The only thing in your way to accomplish this task is you and your setting time aside to get this part done.

Anytime you give a new talk or have been given a new time frame for a talk, you'll want to practice. You can time yourself until you get a feel for what you can share within that allotted time frame. Your confidence will be 10 times stronger when you know that you can share your message clearly and that you

Get more speaking gigs when you train at GetSpeakingGigsNow.com ...

have plenty of time to share your call to action as well.

Q: How do you go about expanding (or shrinking) your talk and why would you want to do this?

Once you have created your learning points and practiced the flow of your presentation, you will want to time yourself.

Initially, I recommend 30 minutes from beginning to end because that is a typical amount of time given for the speaker. From there, you can expand on any of the learning points with case studies, stories, examples, statistics, or exercises to increase the length of the talk. You may also decide to add 1-2 more learning points.

If you need to shrink it down to 15-20 minutes, I recommend keeping the learning points very succinct and increase your level of practice as you will have less wiggle room to get off track. I have found that the less time I have, the more I need to practice so that I stay on point and develop a rhythm for that time frame.

Q: How do you repurpose your talk and why would you want to do this?

We will discuss the concept of repurposing your talk more thoroughly in this book upcoming, but let me explain what repurposing means and why it is beneficial here.

Repurposing is the act of taking something you've created (in this scenario) and using the same content for something else.

For example, I have a talk that I give called, "Get Your Talk Ready to Rock." I also offer a "Get Your Talk Ready to Rock" 1/1 session for people who want to make sure their talk is catered to their style that they can give with confidence and is monetizable. So,

Network with other speakers! Go to GetSpeakingGigsNow.com/network

I have taken the same concepts and content and utilized them to educate audiences and my clients in different ways. The overarching concepts are the same, but the way in which the information is delivered varies.

That is an example of repurposing your content.

This is a valuable lesson because I have met COUNTLESS speakers (authors / coaches) who continue to create new content. They will tell me they got asked to speak and now they need to create a new talk. That is a LOT of time spent on content writing (which could be spent on gaining new clients and serving them).

It is easy to get stuck in the content creation trap. Being in the trap feels good because it seems like you're being productive. But if you stay there too long, your sales dry up and before you know it, you have the best content in the world with no one to hear it.

In other words, remember to utilize the content you have already worked so hard at creating before you jump into a new project.

More to come on repurposing later!

PART II

CREATE YOUR IDEAL SPEAKING GIG PIPELINE

Get more speaking gigs when you train at GetSpeakingGigsNow.com ...

Q: What is a "speaking gig pipeline?"

Oftentimes, speakers do not always have sales experience, but a pipeline is a very common sales term. In the simplest terms, it means your prospects (e.g., potential clients, customers, etc.).

A pipeline is the lifeline to your sales. For this topic, your SALES = SPEAKING GIGS. In order to have a healthy pipeline, you will need many prospects because prospects are what turn into sales.

For example, if you wanted to speak to ABC Chamber of Commerce, that would become your prospect. Ideally you would find out the contact information of the person at that Chamber. That Chamber is now in your pipeline as a prospect. Once you book that Chamber as a speaking gig, it has become a sale.

Q: How do you clarify or define your speaking vision?

- How many engagements do you want?
- What type of audience can you serve best?
- Where would your prospective clients be?

Q: How do you identify your ideal target market for building your speaking gig pipeline?

Even if you have never spoken publicly YET, you can still create a vision of what it would look like. You probably have some idea of the people that you can best serve as a speaker.

Network with other speakers! Go to GetSpeakingGigsNow.com/network

Think of who you really love working with. Who do you know (or predict) will benefit most from what you have to offer?

What is the ideal _____ of your audience?

- Size _____
- Age _____
- Religion / Special Interest _____
- Industry _____
- Language spoken _____
- Culture _____
- Geographical location _____
- Employment status _____
- Other _____

Q: What are some strategies you can use to get your list of speaking gig prospects started?

- Start with warm / familiar market (a.k.a., people who already know you)
  - Who are your raving fans?
  - Who is in your social network?
- Ask people what groups they belong to that invite speakers.
- Post on social media that you are a speaker.
- Optional: Hire Virtual Assistant (VA) to do your research for you.
- LESS THAN A V.A.!!! A "done-for-you" resource that has

Get more speaking gigs when you train at GetSpeakingGigsNow.com ...

the contact information for events / places that invite guest speakers to speak broken down by regions ... **www.GetSpeakingGigsNow.com/Cities**

Q: How do you go about developing a booking strategy that keeps your speaking gig pipeline full?

Just like I suggested having a vision for your speaking, you'll want to have a clear strategy in place to stay booked. That means getting clear on the time and resources you can dedicate to the process AND clarity on the benefits you will receive from your speaking gigs.

Quantity of talks:

How many talks do you envision giving ...

- Annually?
- Monthly?
- Weekly?
- What is your bandwidth for giving X amount of talks?

Q: Let's Talk $$$$$$$$ ... What is your target financial goal for your speaking?

- How much income are you ideally wanting from your talks?
- How many "sales" do you anticipate at each talk?
- What is each sale worth to you approximately?
- How many talks do you need to hit your number?

Network with other speakers! Go to GetSpeakingGigsNow.com/network

Q: What is the #1 quality needed to get booked and stay booked?

CONSISTENCY! Kind of boring, right? You might think it's creativity, intelligence or brilliance, but consistency is what is needed the most.

WHY? If you have the most brilliant talk (story, or expertise) but no one knows about it, you aren't able to make the impact you desire.

Is it important to have an excellent talk and a high level of expertise? YES, but don't lose sight of having consistent systems in place to get you in front of the right audiences.

Oftentimes, I will hear from speakers who are "so busy" providing services and speaking that they don't have time to prospect for speaking engagements. Then they are a little shell-shocked when they realize their calendar is blank and they have no speaking engagements booked.

It is critical that you have systems that work for you, for your business and that you bring in support when your plate gets too full to manage it. There are lots of ways to build your business to suit your needs. But creating consistency in keeping your pipeline full and flowing is the difference between speaking and NOT speaking.

My suggestion is to figure out your systems for prospecting and follow them. Adjust your systems as your business grows, and as you see what you actually do. What is the best system??? The one that you FOLLOW!

Get more speaking gigs when you train at GetSpeakingGigsNow.com ...

Here are some questions to start creating your prospecting strategy:

1. How much time will you set aside for curating your prospect list?

2. What is the best day(s) of the week for you to prospect?

3. What is the best time of day for you to prospect?

4. What does your follow-up system look like?

5. What will you say in your phone calls / emails?

6. How will you manage your calendar for prospecting, administration, sales, speaking and providing services?

Q: What support can you bring in to assist you so that you can do what you're best at?

Once you've devised a plan for yourself, try it out for 2-4 weeks. Make any adjustments needed so that you stay on track with your goals. If you notice that you are putting something on the calendar, but not doing it, it's time to re-evaluate. Remember to celebrate your wins!

Get more speaking gigs when you train at GetSpeakingGigsNow.com ...

PART III

MONETIZE YOUR SPEAKING ENGAGEMENTS

Get more speaking gigs when you train at GetSpeakingGigsNow.com ...

PART III – MONETIZE YOUR SPEAKING ENGAGEMENTS

Q: What are some ways you can monetize your speaking engagements?

There are several ways you can monetize your presentation, which I'll get to in a moment. First, in order to monetize your speaking engagements, you'll need to address these key areas:

MONETIZATION VISION

Your monetization vision is very powerful. What I mean by your monetization vision is what you can IMAGINE happening; meaning, what do you ideally want to happen, NOT what you're worried might happen, but specifically, when it comes to <u>money coming into your life through speaking</u>.

When creating this vision, you will be utilizing several of your senses in your vision - not only what you SEE, but also consider what you would HEAR and FEEL. Basically, you want to get a sense of the whole experience. What will it be like?

Ok, here we go …

YOUR MONETIZATION VISION

Focus on the money coming in to you from your speaking engagements.

Imagine … you are speaking to your ideal groups of potential clients … and you bring in new clients through speaking.

IMAGINE HOW YOU RECEIVE THE MONEY

- Who comes up to you afterwards?

Network with other speakers! Go to GetSpeakingGigsNow.com/network

- What do you hear people say to you?
- How do they pay you?
- Imagine seeing the money in your account.
- Imagine seeing the notification on your phone that money just came to you.
- See the money or checks in your hand.
- What do you hear yourself say internally?
- How do you feel when this is happening?

MONETIZATION PLAN

Your monetization plan consists of knowing (or estimating when you first start out) your numbers. This is your business! You need to start tracking your numbers so that you have an idea of how many speaking engagements you need to hit your financial goals.

Knowing your numbers gives you peace of mind and a level of discernment in knowing what engagements to say yes or no to.

What numbers do you need to know as a speaker?

The first step is to start with what you think is possible and then stair-step it up from there.

Imagine you give 1 TALK a month to your desired audience.

1. If you attracted one client from each talk, what would that equate to in $$$?

Get more speaking gigs when you train at GetSpeakingGigsNow.com ...

2. Dream a little ... how many clients do you imagine you could attract at each talk?

3. Multiply the # of clients you could attract by the amount you charge one client and what do you get?

Now, you have an idea of the financial benefits you will receive from becoming a speaker. You may also see that you need to raise your rates :) AND you may also see that you will attract more clients than you originally thought! That's a very exciting realization!

Once you have some talks under your belt, you'll want to track how many people attended the talk, how many prospects you gained and how many of those prospects turned into clients (and ultimately, what did that mean in dollars sold). This is a basic tracking system for your sales. Knowing these numbers (vs. sticking your head in the sand) will give you incredible insight into where you need to make adjustments along the way.

WAYS TO MONETIZE YOUR TALK

When it comes to monetizing your talk, you can:

- Give an Offer on Stage
- Build Your List & Sell Online
- Sell Products / Services
- Get Speaking Referrals
- Schedule Appointments / Calls
- Host a Webinar

Network with other speakers! Go to GetSpeakingGigsNow.com/network

- Put on a Workshop
- Guest on a Podcast

After looking at the above list of ideas on ways to monetize your talk, what stands out for you? What could you put into place or practice right away to start monetizing your talks? Do it! Also, what other ideas come to mind when it comes to monetizing your talk? Write them out below:

_____

_____

_____

_____

CREATE YOUR MONETIZATION MENU

By this, I mean you will want to have several options of what you can offer or what your CTA (Call-To-Action) is at your talks.

Why? Because not all talks follow the same rules. Some venues will allow you to "make an offer" (a.k.a., sell something) while some will not. You may have 20 minutes to talk. You might have 60 minutes.

The group of people might vary. No biggie. This is part of the game. All you need to do is prepare for it. Have a plan, a

PART III – MONETIZE YOUR SPEAKING ENGAGEMENTS

MONETIZATION MENU, prepared ahead of time so that you are not scrambling the night before with your sales plan.

Let me be clear, the monetization menu is pretty much for your eyes only. This is a behind-the-scenes tool for you to have. YOU get to choose from the menu that YOU created.

Based on the information you have about the venue, you will choose off of the menu. You might decide to have an option for venues that allow you to sell vs. venues that don't. Perhaps you have a different offer for a 20-minute talk vs. a 60-minute talk.

PART IV

SYSTEMS TO GETTING ASKED BACK AGAIN & AGAIN

Get more speaking gigs when you train at GetSpeakingGigsNow.com ...

Q: How do you get asked back again and again when it comes to getting more speaking gigs?

This is probably the most UNDER talked about part of the speaking industry. I think it's not discussed because there is an assumption of common sense.

BUT, after seeing lots of violations (or just innocent unawareness), I'm here to tell you there are EASY ways to get asked back again and again.

Assuming you are a good speaker with good content, what are the TWO most important qualities you should have if you want to get asked back again and again as a speaker?

CONSIDERATION

- Be reliable.
- Be honest.
- Be early.
- Be prepared.

COLLABORATION

- Play nice with others.
- Have a win-win mentality.

Meeting organizers really want to have a great event. They want the audience to enjoy themselves and come back! Having a speaker who is easy to work with, reliable and early makes them much more likely to ask you back.

There are very well-known speakers in the industry who have tarnished reputations due to how they treat the meeting organizers. There are only so many people you can walk all over before it catches up to you.

This is certainly an area that you have fully in your hands to control, so show up with these qualities for every interaction (e.g., the initial phone call, the confirmation calls, the event and the post-event communications) with these qualities in the forefront of your mind.

To ensure you are able to be reliable, on-time, early and prepared, create the following checklist whenever you book a gig:

Booking a Gig Checklist

1. Date
2. Venue
3. Address / Virtual Meeting Link
4. Contact Information
5. Time the Meeting Starts /Ends
6. Time Allotted for Speaking
7. Audio/Visual
8. Additional Notes
9. Approximate Number of Attendees Expected

What else comes to mind that you might want to add to the list that pertains to your specific talk? Add it!

_____

_____

PART IV – SYSTEMS TO GET ASKED BACK AGAIN

EMPLOY a Detailed Checklist for the "Day of" presentation

It's also helpful to have a checklist the day of your presentation. That list might look like this one below. Feel free to customize this list for your needs.

"Day of" Checklist: <u>Sales / Marketing</u>

- Clarity on Monetization Plan
- Any Registration Forms / Handouts
- Items / Products You are Selling
- Payment Plan Breakdown
- A Way to Take Money
- Business Cards
- Pens / Clipboards if Needed
- Banners
- Tripod for Video Taping
- Reminder to Have Someone Take Photos / Video
- Post Event to Social Media
- Links / Slides with your "Call To Action"

"Day of" Checklist <u>Technology</u>

- Laptop

- Clicker
- Extra batteries for clicker
- Power Cord
- HDMI Cord / Adaptors for Projector
- Thumbdrive

"Day of" Checklist: <u>Delivery</u>

- Print Out of Your PowerPoint
- Easel / Markers
- Materials Needed to Deliver Presentation (e.g., AV, etc.)
- Speaker Introduction Sheet
- Check Travel Time
- Attire

Q: What are some essential "must-haves" or "must take with you" items to bring to every speaking gig?

FIRST: If NOTHING else … make sure you can deliver your talk no matter what. For example, if the lights go out and the only way you can deliver your talk is with a PowerPoint, then you are screwed and your opportunity is wasted. Do whatever you need to do to make sure you can deliver your message regardless of the circumstances.

Get more speaking gigs when you train at GetSpeakingGigsNow.com ...

I have seen hard drives fried, thumb drives erased mysteriously, electricity go out, missing laptops, every kind of technical snafu you can imagine!

The SHOW MUST GO ON! Your ability to deliver your message through PRACTICE and PREPARATION is 1,000,000% in your hands.

SECOND: I'm saying this clearly here in case you didn't assume it in the above section. You MUST have a way to accept sales (assuming you are utilizing speaking as a way to gain clients or generate money).

I have seen SO many speakers LOSE out big time on this opportunity because they were so focused on the content portion of their talk, the sales part just slipped their mind.

OUCH!

This hurts me when I see this. All of the work and planning and time that went into getting the gig, preparing for the gig, being at the gig … only to walk away with nothing because of lack of planning. SO painful to see! Don't let that be you! Make sure you have a plan.

Q: What other checklist(s) should you create if you plan on being a professional speaker booking a lot of speaking gigs?

I suggest having a checklist for your technology needs and your content delivery. Plan to bring EVERYTHING that you might need. It is much better to bring it and not need it than to need it and not have it! Store an office box of extra cables, adapters and extension cords, for example.

Network with other speakers! Go to GetSpeakingGigsNow.com/network

Q: How do you plan for flexibility when you're a speaker?

Planning for flexibility depends heavily on your mindset as a speaker. Stepping into ANY speaking situation will involve things out of your hands to control. However, your attitude is IN your hands to control. Knowing ahead of time that certain unexpected obstacles can happen will keep you calm in the moment.

Ideally, you will have prepared ahead of time with the meeting planner. For example, you may have an idea of what the venue environment is like, how much time is allotted for your talk and the type of people who will be there. You can find out if there is going to be food served during the time you'll be speaking, etc.

But sometimes, even with the most preparation, things get miscommunicated, people are running behind, there is more noise than anticipated, etc. The biggest way to plan for flexibility is to speak to what's happening in the room and then just "go with it."

For example, one time I was leading a talk in a business that had a big warehouse. There were about 50 people packed into the warehouse and unfortunately there was no air conditioning. (Imagine a hot California summer night.) So, they had the warehouse garage door open. Little did I know that the train tracks were right outside.

So every once in awhile, a train would pass by. There was no point in trying to talk over the sound of the train, so I addressed the noise (after the first time it passed) and we agreed to take a moment of reflection the next time a train passed.

Get more speaking gigs when you train at GetSpeakingGigsNow.com ...

PART V

SPEAKER SHEET DEVELOPMENT YOU'LL NEED

Q: What is a "speaker sheet?"

A speaker sheet is a sales page for you as a speaker. It is also referred to as a:

- One Sheet
- Speaker One Sheet
- Speaker Page
- Speaker One Page

They are all referencing the same thing.

Your speaker sheet comprises all of your pertinent information as a speaker. It is for the host or meeting planner or organizer. Ideally, it highlights you as a speaker and is utilized as a tool to increase your credibility and odds of getting booked to speak.

Q: How many "speaker sheets" do you need?

This is dependent on the individual. If you have different business or markets that you target, then you would want to create different speaker sheets for each niche you speak in.

For example, one of my clients speaks for corporate conferences and conventions as a paid speaker who travels. But when she's not travelling she loves to speak on more heart centered topics to women's groups in her local area.

She serves both types of clients and has talks developed for both types of audiences. But the speaker sheet she sends is very different depending on which group she's targeting.

Q: What goes into making a "speaker sheet?"

A speaker sheet will be a reflection of you as a speaker and should be branded to match all of your other marketing materials. I highly, highly, highly recommend you utilize a graphic designer for this project. This will be one of the documents you will use MOST as a speaker, so you want to really shine! When they design it, ask that they give you the original file so you can make future edits.

To get this done, all you have to do is research online and gather 3-5 speaker sheets you admire and let the graphic designer do their job at creating yours. Replace the content, photos and contact information on those sample one-sheets with yours, naturally.

Q: How do "speaker sheets" help you get speaker gigs?

Having a speaker sheet has both intrinsic and extrinsic benefits to getting you booked.

Intrinsic Benefits ... to having a speaker sheet:

Your confidence skyrockets when you have all of your ducks in a row. You want to have a high level of certainty and confidence when you are marketing yourself as a speaker. You want to have high credibility and to be taken seriously.

Extrinsic Benefits ... to having a speaker sheet:

By having your speaker sheet, you are demonstrating that

PART V – SPEAKER SHEET DEVELOPMENT YOU'LL NEED 41

your topics are developed and tested. You have experience as a speaker, and this gives the booker confidence that you are going to show up and deliver.

I have had many speakers tell me they are a great speaker and then I ask them to send me their speaker sheet and what do I get? Excuses, or worse ... crickets! That shows me they haven't put their stake in the ground or prepared themselves in such a way that best (and most easily) represents themselves. They aren't invested in their speaker services and skills enough to take that extra step and package themselves as a speaker with the use of a speaker one-sheet.

TAKE ACTION: Here's a checklist to help you get started with you creating your speaker one-sheet:

1. **Research online and find 3-5 speaker one-sheets** you really like. Just look up "speaker one-sheet" or "speaker one-sheet templates" and click on the Images tab in the search window. What do you see? Download those you like to your computer. You'll be giving those to your graphic designer.

2. **If you don't know a graphic designer, go to Fiverr.com and search for "create speaker one-sheet"** and see who pops up. Read through 3-5 of them, looking at their rates, ratings, turn-around time and samples from past clients. Then, take the plunge.

3. **Using a Word or Google document,** gather up contact information, a 1-2 paragraph bio about yourself, and a list of topics you can speak on or one topic with a list of benefits your intended audiences will learn when they hear

Network with other speakers! Go to GetSpeakingGigsNow.com/network

you speak. You can also insert 2-3 short testimonials about your presentation too, if you like.

4. **Find your best head shot** and one action shot, if you have one, to put on this speaker one-sheet.

5. **Send all this information** and files to your graphic designer via email (attachments) to help them get started.

That's pretty much how you get started creating your speaker one-sheet. Now, you have no excuses why you can't get this done. I've laid it all out for you step-by-step.

PART VI

KEEPING YOUR SPEAKING GIG PIPELINE FULL

Get more speaking gigs when you train at GetSpeakingGigsNow.com ...

PART VI – KEEPING YOUR SPEAKING GIG PIPELINE FULL   45

Q: What is a speaking gig pipeline and how do you keep it FULL?

As a reminder, we introduced the concept of pipelines in PART 2. Oftentimes, speakers do not always have sales experience, but a pipeline is a very common sales term. In the simplest of terms, a pipeline means your prospects (i.e., potential clients, customers, etc.). A pipeline is the lifeline to your sales. For this topic, your SALES = SPEAKING GIGS. In order to have a healthy pipeline, you will need many prospects because prospects are what turn into sales.

For example, if you wanted to speak to ABC Chamber of Commerce, that would become your prospect. Ideally you would find out the contact information of the person at that Chamber. That Chamber is now in your pipeline as a prospect. Once you book that Chamber as a speaking gig, it has become a sale.

Q: How do you create a speaking gig pipeline?

The easiest method to create your speaking gig pipeline is to start with your warm market.

Q: What is a warm market?

These are people you already know. People who already know, like and trust you. Maybe you are related to them (don't disregard your family and who they know) or worked with in a past job. This could be friends from high school or college, previous clients, people you know through networking, neighbors, vendors, people you meet at other speaking events, etc. The average person knows 300 people. Now with social media, you probably know a LOT more than that!

Network with other speakers! Go to GetSpeakingGigsNow.com/network

Develop a strategy to let your warm market know that you are speaking now and give them an idea of what your area of expertise is. Don't go writing a novel here; keep it short and to the point. You can even show them your speaker one-sheet. That's something they can pass along to those they know who might get you booked to speak.

Once you've tapped into your warm market, you can create new contacts via networking, social media, or cold calling organizations (my least favorite, but it does work).

When cold calling, just call up an organization and ask this very simple question, "Do you need speakers to come speak to your group and what type of speakers do you like to have come speak?" Done. Simple.

Most people who receive your phone call might be glad you called. "Yes, we do have speakers come. What do you speak about? Maybe I can pass your topic around to our group and see if they'd like you to come and speak. Do you have A SPEAKER ONE-SHEET we can pass around?" NOT that they know to call it that, but do you see the importance of having that one-sheet? "Let me get your email and I'll send you my speaker one-sheet that can answer many of your questions and get people excited about having me come and speak."

The idea is that you start to let the world know what you're up to. I have gotten incredible referrals from non-business related relationships. For example, my mom is one of my biggest referrers! I also spoke a very well-known medical company because of a referral from a neighbor at a barbecue party. Knowing that leads can come from anywhere, your job is simple … BE PREPARED to turn them into SALES (i.e., a booked speaking gig).

Get more speaking gigs when you train at GetSpeakingGigsNow.com …

Q: How do you utilize a speaking gig pipeline to get booked as a speaker?

Once you get your pipeline filled up, you'll want to utilize some type of tracking system (no, post-it's don't count!). In the sales industry we call this a CRM (Client/Customer Relationship Manager).

This way you will have a place to house all of your contacts and create a reminder task list of when to reach out to them next. Otherwise, those golden opportunities will fall through the cracks and you will wonder why you have to keep finding new prospects.

Q: How do you keep growing your speaking gig pipeline?

The easiest way to grow your speaking gig pipeline once you've gotten it started is to LEVERAGE and REPURPOSE your talks.

Here's what I mean by LEVERAGING your talk:

If you are already at your talk and you have a relationship with the meeting organizer, you will want to create:

- Opportunities to get booked again in the future

- Speaking referrals from audience members

- Testimonials from the event

- Publicity from the event (e.g., social media posts, video, posting on your website, emailing your list, etc.)

Network with other speakers! Go to GetSpeakingGigsNow.com/network

Here's what I mean by REPURPOSE your talk:

Many times I will hear speakers stressed out about writing new content. They haven't realized the power of repurposing the content they already wrote. For example, if you get asked to be on a podcast or radio show, there is no need for you to create new content.

Instead, you can utilize the content of your talk to shape the questions the interviewer will use for the podcast or radio show.

You can repurpose your speaking content into:

- Videos
- Blog Articles
- Vlogs
- Magazine Articles
- Social Media Posts
- Podcasts
- Webinars
- Live Streaming Events

… and so much more!

Get more speaking gigs when you train at GetSpeakingGigsNow.com …

PART VII

SCRIPTS FOR GETTING BOOKED & STAYING BOOKED

Get more speaking gigs when you train at GetSpeakingGigsNow.com ...

PART VII – SCRIPTS FOR GETTING BOOKED

Q: What are "scripts" for getting booked and staying booked?

Most sales professionals used a script when they first got started. It's a guideline or template you can use to make sure you cover all of the appropriate questions and topics needed in the conversation in order to "get the sale."

In this scenario, the "sale" is the speaking engagement.

Q: How do you come up with a speaking (or speaker's) script?

The best way to come up with your script is to:

1. Write up a list of questions you would want to ask a prospect.

2. Write up a short list of items you would need to communicate to the prospect.

3. Read them out loud to see if they sound natural.

4. Edit them as needed to match your personality. Remember, you will be speaking these words, so it can't sound canned or memorize.

5. Practice until you feel like you have a natural rhythm down.

Q: How do you use a speaker script to GET booked?

1. Once you have practiced your script and feel comfortable and confident, have it nearby so you can reference it if needed during your conversation.

2. When you make contact with a prospect on the phone, you

can use your script as a guideline (until you get comfortable enough not to need it anymore).

3. Use your script to make sure you've gotten the pertinent information needed to see if there is a match between you and the speaking gig.

4. Remember, you're talking to a human being - don't be canned and stilted. If you sound too memorized or scripted, you will likely get a "no." The key is to sound confident, disarming, and natural.

Q: How do you use (or apply) speaker scripts to STAY booked?

Initially, you are booking brand new (to you) speaking gigs. However, as you book those, you'll have the opportunity to book those initial venues again for a future gig.

Types of Scripts to STAY booked:

- Thank you note (for after the gig is complete) ...
- Keeping in touch ...
- Suggesting a new topic for a future gig ...

Q: Do scripts change over time?

I have found that the same script I used when I booked my first gig is pretty much the same as what I say now.

What HAS changed is my confidence over time. Since I've had so many speaking gigs (and hundreds of conversations about speaking gigs) I have developed an unconscious competence

Get more speaking gigs when you train at GetSpeakingGigsNow.com ...

and so will you. Trust me, it gets easier each time you do it.

Reasons your script might change:

- You wrote a book ...

- You added a new service that is pertinent to the conversation ...

- You shifted your topic / area of expertise ...

- You have changed your speaking strategy (i.e., the type of audience, venue, etc.) ...

- The degree to which you know the person on the phone (i.e., someone you know vs. a stranger) ...

Q: What else should you know about scripts?

- When you are wanting to land a speaking engagement, the first thing you want to do is to find out if it's a match.

- Don't READ your script when you're talking to someone, as most people find that to be a HUGE turn-off!

- Use them as a GUIDELINE so you cover what's needed to get booked and have an amazing event.

- You probably won't need it after you book your first 20 gigs.

- Use the scripts to develop your unconscious competence in the area of having a booking conversation.

LEISA REID

SUMMARY WRAP-UP!

GET SPEAKING GIGS SUMMARY WRAP-UP!

WOW! You have just learned A LOT about getting booked and staying booked as a speaker. I hope you are as inspired as I felt writing this book for you.

As I have mentioned before, speaking is an exciting field! There are no limits to what you can do. Your willingness to get out there and share your message is to be commended.

It takes a lot of courage to be the one standing on that stage, but when I think about all of the people you will impact and the ripple effect your message will create, I get goosebumps!

If you liked this book and want more tips and resources for becoming a rock star speaker, head on over to my website:

www.GetSpeakingGigsNow.com

In advance, here's to your speaking success!

Genuinely,

Leisa Reid

LEISA REID
FOUNDER / TRAINER
GetSpeakingGigsNow.com

Network with other speakers! Go to GetSpeakingGigsNow.com/network

SPEAKER RESOURCES & MORE

LEISA'S OTHER BOOK

Manage to Success: A Guide to Cultivating Happy and Productive Employees by Leisa Reid

There is a huge gap in management training today. Managers are thrown into positions because they know the job, but they get little to no training on how to cultivate happy and productive employees. How do you successfully manage your employees when there is literally no training program and you feel like you have no time? The key is to become your own advocate and educate yourself, so you can live a balanced life and become an extraordinary leader.

SPEAKER'S TRAINING ACADEMY

If you like what you read inside **Get Speaking Gigs Now**, then you'll want to check out the Speaker's Training Academy where Leisa goes more in depth in all of the following key areas of getting more speaking gigs:

1. Get Your Talk Ready to Rock
2. Create Your Ideal Speaking Gig Pipeline
3. Monetize Your Speaking Engagements
4. Systems To Getting Asked Back Again & Again
5. Speaker Sheet Development You'll Need
6. Keeping Your Speaking Gig Pipeline FULL
7. Scripts For Getting Booked & Staying Booked

www.GetSpeakingGigsNow.com

SPEAKERCAFE.COM

DIRECTORY "PROFILE LISTING"

WHAT IS IT? Directory profile listings on **SpeakerCafe.com** quickly and publicly showcase your speaker services as the expert to call on to be booked as a speaker for someone's upcoming event or need for a speaker.

WHY HAVE A PROFILE LISTING ON SPEAKERCAFE.COM? While most websites get lost like grains of sand on a beach, SpeakerCafe.com profiles stand out to those looking to find speakers for their events. Sure, they could go to your website IF they knew about you. What most event planners like to do is stop by SpeakerCafe.com real quick to see if there's a speaker that fits their needs. If you don't have a listing on SpeakerCafe.com, then you're guaranteed not to be seen or booked.

WHAT DO YOU GET WITH YOUR SPEAKERCAFE.COM LISTING? While there are different membership levels you can subscribe to, in general, every member gets to publicly display all of the following to help win the minds of potential TV show personnel decision-makers looking to book TV guests for their TV shows. You get to display:

- ★ Name / Title / Profession
- ★ Contact Info (Phone# / email)
- ★ Bio / About / Description
- ★ Post Speaking Topics
- ★ Upload Audio & Video
- ★ Upload Articles & Photos

SELF-MANAGED SPEAKERCAFE.COM PROFILE LISTINGS: That's right! You get to create, login and maintain your own profile listing yourself. This is perfect when you want to add more content to your profile listing, such as new videos, photos and articles, update your contact info, etc.

SpeakerCafe.com PROFILE LISTING COST: While we are always running specials, if you consider this an investment into making you more money and getting you more exposure, write this off as a tax-deductible advertising expense and get listed today!

www.SpeakerCafe.com

SAMPLE SPEAKERCAFE.COM DIRECTORY PROFILE LISTING

Your Name

Professional Speaker
YourWebsite.com
Your Town, ST 00000

📞 CALL (000) 000-0000

Contact This Speaker   **Review This Speaker**

💬 MAKE A CONNECTION! Your Name would like to hear from you. **Contact This Speaker!**

BIO   TOPICS   AUDIENCES   PHOTOS   VIDEOS   TESTIMONIALS

Contact Information:

Website	http://YourWebsite.com
Social Profiles	[icons]
Telephone	000-000-0000
One-Sheet	View My Speaker One-Sheet / Brochure
Travels From	Your Town, State
Credentials	Enter your credentials, awards, recognition statements, accomplishments, etc., in your field of experience or experience to impress potential companies/organizations looking to book you as a speaker.

GET YOUR LISTING TODAY!

MEET (YOUR NAME)

ENTER YOUR SPEAKING TOPICS
that you would like to speak on ...

Write 1-2 paragraphs that describe a problem out in the world and perhaps what's not being done about it. This problem/topic is what you want to be interviewed on because you're the expert that can solve this problem, shed light on it, explain it better, set the record straight, etc.

- List how people are suffering from this problem ...
- What's common among people with this problem ...

Again, this is just a sample SpeakerCafe.com DIRECTORY PROFILE LISTING that gives companies the info they need and on ONE PAGE to decide if you're the perfect speaker for their next event! <u>GET YOUR LISTING TODAY!</u>

www.SpeakerCafe.com

"PROFILE LISTING" CATEGORIES

These categories represent niche subjects companies and organizations need speakers for. Peruse these categories. Could you speak effectively on any one (or more) of these topics? If so, get your directory listing today so you can be seen tomorrow by those looking to book speakers for their next event.

ADD & ADHD
Abuse
Accountability
Achievement
Addiction / Recovery
Adoption / Fostering
Adult Entertainment
Adventurers
Advertising
African-American
Aging / Anti-Aging
Alcoholism
American History
American Legends
Anger Management
Animals
Archaeology
Art Performances
Arts & Pop Culture
Athletics / Sports
Attitude
Author
Autism
Awareness & Prevention
Body Language
Branding
Bullying
Business
Business Building
Business Entrepreneurship
Business Growth
Business Trends
Business of Healthcare
Cancer
Cancer Awareness
Career
Celebrity
Celebrity Chefs
Celebrity Speakers
Change
Character Portrayals
China
Christian
Chronic Diseases
Cirque / Acrobats
Coaching
College/University
Comedy
Communication
Communities
Community Relations
Competition
Conflict Resolution
Construction / Building
Consulting
Consumer Trends
Corporate Culture
Corporate Responsibility
Corporate Social Responsibility
Creativity
Crisis
Cultural
Cultural Diversity
Customer Service
Dental Health / Tooth Care
Difficult People
Disability Issues
Disaster Recovery
Domestic Violence
Drug Abuse
Eating Disorders
Ecommerce / Online Sales
Economy
Education
Elementary Education
Emotional Balance
Employees / Workforce
Empowerment
Energy (Oil, Gas, etc.)
Entertainment
Entrepreneurship
Environmental
Environmental Policy
Ethics & Values
Etiquette
Exercise / Fitness
Facilitator
Family
Finance & Insurance
Financial Freedom
Food
Franchising
Freedom
Fundraising
Futurists
Gender Issues
Generation Issues
Global Business
Global Issues
Goal Setting
Government/Politics
Green Issues / Living
Grief
HIV, Aids & STD
Happiness
Health
Health & Beauty
Health & Nutrition

Healthcare Experts	Networking	Social Media
Healthy Lifestyle	News & Current Events	Social Services
History	Nutrition	Spirituality
Home & Garden	Olympic Athletes	Sports
Home Health / Care Giving	Organizational Skills	Spouse Programs
Homeland Security	Overcoming Adversity	Strategic Planning
Human / Sex Trafficking	Parenting & Children	Stress & Anxiety
Human Resources	Patriotism	Success
Humor	Peak Performance	Succession Planning
Identity Theft & Safety	Performance Improvement	Suicide Awareness
Image / Self Esteem	Personal / Life Coaching	Sustainability
Innovation & Creativity	Personal Development	TED Conference
Inspiration	Personal Safety	TEDX Conference
International Affairs	Personality Testing	Tax Planning
Internet / World Wide Web	Pets	Team Building
Internet Marketing	Photography	Technology
Investing / Financial Issues	Political	Teens
Judicial System	Political Humor	Time Management
Language	Presentation Skills	Top News
Law	Productivity	Travel/Tourism
Law of Attraction	Profitability	Vaccines
Leadership	Prosperity	Videography
Learning Disorders	Psychology	Vision / Eyesight
Life After Work	Publicity / Public Relations	Vision / Purpose
Life At Work	Real Estate	Volunteerism
Life Balance	Reality TV Stars	Web Design
Lifestyle	Recruitment & Retention	Weight Loss
Listening Skills	Relationships	Wellness
Magic / Illusion	Religion	Women
Management	Restaurant Industry	Women In Business
Marketing	Retail	Women In Society
Master of Ceremonies	Retirement / Aging	Work/Life Balance
Media	Revues & Variety Shows	Workplace Safety
Medical	Risk Management	Writing
Men	Safety	Youth Issues
Mental Health	Sales	
Mentalists & Hypnotists	Science & Engineering	
Metaphysics	Security	
Midlife Transitions	Self Empowerment	
Military	Self Help	
Military / Veterans	Self-Publishing	
Mind / Body Medicine	Sex & Sensuality	
Money Mindset	Sex Education	
Motivation	Sexual Abuse	
NLP	Small Business	
Negotiation	Social Causes	

GET YOUR **LISTING** TODAY!

ON **SpeakerCafe.com**

"PROFILE LISTING" CONTENT

What do you get to advertise/showcase publicly in front of hundreds, if not thousands, of potential companies looking to book speakers for their next event? With your **SpeakerCafe.com directory profile listing**, you get to add all of the following to your profile to showcase your speaking talents. For example, you can showcase:

- ☑ YOUR **FULL NAME**
- ☑ YOUR **COMPANY NAME**
- ☑ YOUR **PHONE NUMBER**
- ☑ YOUR **WEBSITE**
- ☑ YOUR **AVAILABILITY**
- ☑ YOUR **SPEAKER FEES**
- ☑ YOUR **CITY/STATE** (LOCATION YOU TRAVEL FROM)
- ☑ YOUR **PHOTO** (PROFESSIONAL HEAD SHOT)
- ☑ YOUR **CREDENTIALS** (EXPERT BIO, DEGREES, ETC.)
- ☑ YOUR **SOCIAL MEDIA ACCOUNTS** (VIA LINKS)
- ☑ **SPEAKING TOPICS/IDEAS** (ONE OR MORE)
- ☑ **SPEAKER TESTIMONIALS** (FROM PAST GIGS)
- ☑ **ARTICLES** (ABOUT YOUR SPEAKING NICHE/TOPICS)
- ☑ **PHOTOS** (SHOWING YOU SPEAKING)
- ☑ **VIDEOS** (SHOWING YOU SPEAKING)
- ☑ **EVENTS** (POST UPCOMING SPEAKING GIGS)

GET YOUR LISTING TODAY!

Pretty much everything you can add to your profile is speaker-related, speaker-focused, and rich with (your) contact information so event planners know how to contact you immediately and without any middle-man taking a % of any paid speaker profits to possibly book you as a speaker for their upcoming event!

"PROFILE LISTING" USES

Now that you know what a **SpeakerCafe.com directory profile listing** looks like, the categories you can align yourself with, in addition to the content you can display to help attract potential companies and organizations to book you to speak, the next question is, **what can you do with your SpeakerCafe directory profile listing**? Well, here are all the ways you can use your SpeakerCafe.com directory profile listing:

☑ USE IT TO **PITCH COMPANIES TO BOOK YOU FOR SPEAKING** — It's easy to pitch practically any company to book you if you have all your speaker-related/speaker-focused information in one place, making it easy to find, easy to read/follow and easy to contact you! Why wouldn't you get booked *in a flash* to be someone's next speaker?

☑ USE IT AS **YOUR RESUME** — Looking to get booked by a potential client? Send them to your **SpeakerCafe.com directory listing**. They can see all your expertise, view your credentials, see sample videos of you speaking, see the topics you speak on, and much more.

☑ USE IT AS **YOUR WEBSITE** — You might like to use your **SpeakerCafe.com directory profile listing** as your actual website. Why? Because it costs A LOT of money to build and maintain an actual website, let alone TIME to build it. Considering the complexity of maintaining a website today, why bother? Just use your **SpeakerCafe directory listing** to showcase what you do, link to your social media accounts, attract clients to book you to speak and much more!

GET YOUR **SPEAKERCAFE DIRECTORY PROFILE LISTING** TODAY! GO TO:

SPEAKERCAFE.COM